MW01017226

# WHEN I LEARNED TO DANCE WITH LIFE

Reverend Wallis Pattisonn

THINK RICH LIVE RICH™

PUBLISHER

Think Rich Live Rich Inc.
2418 Thurston Ave NE,
Olympia WA 98506
Tel: (360)352-4988
www.thinkrichliverich.com

**Ordering Information:**
**Quantity Sales:** Special discounts are available on quantity purchases by corporations, Associations, and others. For details contact "Special Sales Department" at the address above. All retail and other Sales are available through the contact details above.

Think Rich Live Rich and the TRLR logo are registered Trademarks of Think Rich Live Rich Inc. Published in the United States of America. Printed in India at **www.devtechprinters.com** on bagasse based (sugar cane waste) eco friendly paper made using renewable raw materials with minimum impact on the environment.

**Library of Congress Cataloging in Publication**
Wallis Pattisonn
When I Learned to Dance With Life.
Taking Responsibility for Myself
Reverend Wallis Pattisonn
**ISBN 978-1-4507-1259-0**

1. Spiritual   2. Values   3. Transformation

Art and design by: www.logicbox.com.pk
First Edition

## ACKNOWLEDGMENT

To my Lois, your life is my gift, I will treasure you always. To my children, and grandchildren, you have taught me to search for a better way. To you Mr. P. I will hold you forever in my heart.

My life, up until I was middle age was full of anger and self recrimination. I played victim in everything that I did and of course life gave me more of what I focused on. Around the time of the third act of my life, I finally gathered enough knowledge and spiritual education to make dramatic changes to my life, and I did. In 2008, I moved across the pond as I call it, from Australia to the United States to begin an extraordinary journey that for the first eighteen months would have me in a heightened state of uncertainty and fear of the unknown. In late 2009, I was certain that life had to change, I wanted so much to see the adventure in life and face whatever life brought along with an attitude of synchronicity and grace. At exactly this time, my vision of a swirling Dervish rose before me and I saw life as a dance, the writings in the following pages are a summary of this life of mine and how I learnt to dance with it. My wish is that when you read this, you will see similarities between your life and mine, realizing that we all face the same uncertainties and fears. The important thing is we can, and do overcome them if we want to. I have reminded myself that I get up, I walk, I fall down, meanwhile I keep dancing.

## I Hope You Dance.

When I learned to dance with life

*I felt a freedom that warmed
my bones  and filled my heart*

When I learned to dance with life

*I knew my life had just begun,*
*there was much to explore and experience*

When I learned to dance with life

*I melted into the great beyond*
*and became a stellar being*

When I learned to dance with life

*I discovered a new me,*
*one that I loved and respected*

When I learned to dance with life

*I cried at the enormity of what I saw I could become*

When I learned to dance with life

*I no longer felt small and insignificant,*
*my new being filled space and time*

When I learned to dance with life

*Every part of me was open to a new*
*and wonderful world*

When I learned to dance with life

*My indwelling spirit gave flight,
it soared like an eagle*

When I learned to dance with life

*I became open to new meanings,*
*I asked myself, was this true?*

When I learned to dance with life

*I became less judgmental of others,*
*I learned to be more accepting*

When I learned to dance with life

*The times when I felt confused,
I remembered my Rabbi, mentor who said,
"Life is about walking and bumping."*

When I learned to dance with life

*I cried so hard with the joy and sorrow,*
*my tear ducts could not cope*

When I learned to dance with life

*I accepted the passing of those dearest to me,*
*letting go was a lesson in knowing and seeing gratitude*

When I learned to dance with life

*I accepted my own mortality,*
*and how precious I am, you are, and time is*

When I learned to dance with life

*All that I believed to be me,
faded away with the realization
of who I really am*

When I learned to dance with life

*Anger and frustration became acceptable,
being imperfect was perfect*

When I learned to dance with life

*I hugged myself so hard,*
*I was out of breath*

When I learned to dance with life

*Everything became*
*a cherished moment in time*

When I learned to dance with life

*Love became the most important
thing in my life*

When I learned to dance with life

*I let go of old habits and beliefs,*
*I found new wonderful ones*

When I learned to dance with life

*I noticed how green the trees are,
how if I listen they talk to me*

When I learned to dance with life

*I cried more, I connected to my soul
at the deepest level of my being*

When I learned to dance with life

*Everything that happened around*
*me became okay*

When I learned to dance with life

*I remembered how great my mum was*
*and how much I love and miss her*

When I learned to dance with life

*My heart opened like a blossoming flower,
allowing the universe to touch me*

When I learned to dance with life

*My hearing improved, I heard people
say interesting and wonderful things*

When I learned to dance with life

*I saw the love in my dog's eyes,*
*their inner self was revealed,*
*they have brought many blessings into my life*

When I learned to dance with life

*My family became human ,*
*I was no longer afraid of them,*
*I accepted them as they are, warts and all*

When I learned to dance with life

*I felt and saw my connectedness*
*to all living things*

open saw realizin

When I learned to dance with life

*I became more open to change,*
*I saw life as an adventure,*
*realizing that nothing is permanent*

When I learned to dance with life

*My garden became my sanctuary,*
*it provided me with solace and comfort*

When I learned to dance with life

*I felt an inner strength I never felt before,
spirit filled my being*

When I learned to dance with life

*Nothing was impossible,*
*possibilities showed up every day,*
*even before breakfast*

When I learned to dance with life

*I wanted to hug the world,*
*and mentally I did*

When I learned to dance with life

*I knew my life was mine, all mine.*
*The responsibility for my dreams,*
*hopes and wishes were mine also*

When I learned to dance with life

*Frustration, fear, and anger became manageable*

When I learned to dance with life

*I experienced love*
*beyond anything I could have imagined*

When I learned to dance with life

*My creativity emerged to say:*
*take me on a wonderful journey*

When I learned to dance with life

*I struggled with the new me for a while,
the old me wanted to remain*

When I learned to dance with life

*I was determined to float downstream,
not swim upstream*

When I learned to dance with life

*I was constantly amazed at the new me,
I loved the new possibilities of what I saw*

When I learned to dance with life

*Ideas came from nowhere,*
*anything and everything became possible*

ance feel
daydream

When I learned to dance with life

*I would sit and feel my thoughts,
allow myself to daydream*

When I learned to dance with life

*I no longer wanted to be all things to all people*

When I learned to dance with life

*I learned to respect myself,*
*only then could I respect others*

spring
endless moments

When I learned to dance with life

*There were endless wonderful moments
in which life opened like a blossoming flower in spring*

When I learned to dance with life

*My path was lit up with a new knowing*

When I learned to dance with life

*I realized how small I am in the scheme of things,*
*and yet how large I am in the eyes of great spirit*

When I learned to dance with life

*Being upset and uncertain today was all okay,*
*tomorrow it would be something else*

When I learned to dance with life

*I went through phases of great uncertainty*
*and realized I am not alone.*
*Don't we all sometimes feel this way?*

When I learned to dance with life

*Being in touch with my indwelling spirit
became the highlighted path*

When I learned to dance with life

*There were times when I became irritated
and wanted to return to my old ways,
it took strength not to turn back*

When I learned to dance with life

*I sometimes lost sight of my direction,
returning from this confusion was
such bliss*

When I learned to dance with life

*I had moments of wanting to shut myself
off from the world, this was okay as I realized it
was my time for respite and reflection*

When I learned to dance with life

*I realized I sometimes watched from a distance
what was going on around me,
what I called detachment was just me processing*

When I learned to dance with life

*I imagined I was a swirling dervish with the*
*warm sand beneath my feet,*
*tickling my toes and making me laugh*

live anywhere
companion

When I learned to dance with life

*I realized I could live anywhere and do
anything without fear.
Faith became a well known companion*

When I learned to dance with life

*Impossibilities became possible,*
*dreams became important*

When I learned to dance with life

*I learned to tune into myself, not tune out*

When I learned to dance with life

*Love, freedom and time became the most*
*cherished things I could have*

When I learned to dance with life

*I stopped worrying about whether life would
give me what I wanted, I learned to let go
and trust that all my needs would be met*

When I learned to dance with life

*Grey feathers kept appearing on my pathway*
*to guide me  on my journey*

oice heart head

When I learned to dance with life

*The voice in my heart became louder than
the voice in my head*

When I learned to dance with life

*This moment, this space, became sacred and blessed*

When I learned to dance with life

*Being accepted by others became a question of,
did I accept myself?*

When I learned to dance with life

*The questions in my head turned to inquiry
and I knew this was better for me*

When I learned to dance with life

*I knew that being irritable with others was*
*only me being annoyed with me*

When I learned to dance with life

*Exciting new challenges showed up continuously*
*to test me and to teach me*

When I learned to dance with life

*The person who I saw in the mirror was
only the external me, who I really am is a matter
for me to discover*

When I learned to dance with life

*It was okay when I did not get invited;*
*the truth is, it was better for me if I didn't*

When I learned to dance with life

*Not finishing a task was not the end of the world*

When I learned to dance with life

*The fact that I had never stuck to one thing,*
*became a blessing,*
*I learned many new and wonderful things by being inquisitive*

When I learned to dance with life

*I saw you not as the enemy, but as my friend,*
*to be respected for who you are,*
*to honor the differences*

When I learned to dance with life

*Being a mother and grandmother was wonderful,
it did not define who I am,
I am limitless, my potential is untapped.*

When I learned to dance with life

*Criticism became an interesting concept,*
*was it about me or you?*

When I learned to dance with life

*Sunsets, the warble of the magpies,
droughts and flooding rains were welcome
reminders of the seasons of life*

When I learned to dance with life

*I allowed myself to share my life and my experiences with whomever wanted to listen*